WRITTEN BY

GW00786334

Life
Every Day

It's a New Dawn

© CWR 2020

Published 2020 by CWR, Waverley Abbey House, Waverley Lane, Farnham, Surrey GU9 8EP, UK

Tel: 01252 784700 Email: mail@waverleyabbeyresources.org

Registered Charity No. 294387 Registered Limited Company No. 1990308

All rights reserved. No part of this publication may be reproduced, stored in a retrieval system, or transmitted, in any form or by any means, electronic, mechanical, photocopying, recording or otherwise, without the prior permission in writing of CWR.

Unless otherwise indicated, all Scripture references are from The Holy Bible, New International Version (Anglicised edition), copyright © 1979, 1984, 2011 by Biblica (formerly International Bible Society).

Concept development, editing, design and production by CWR.

Front cover image: blackdiamond67

Printed in the UK by Linney.

FSC
www.fsc.org

MIX
Paper from
responsible sources
FSC® C015900

Waverley Abbey
RESOURCES

Trading name of **CWR**

How to get the best out of *Life Every Day*

HERE ARE A FEW SUGGESTIONS:

- Ideally, carve out a regular time and place each day, with as few distractions as possible. Ask God what He has to say to you.

- Read the Bible passages suggested in the 'Read' references. (As tempting as it is, try not to skip the Bible reading and get straight into the notes.)

- The 'Focus' reference then gives you one or two verses to look at in more detail. Consider what the reading is saying to you and what challenges that may bring.

- Each day's comments are part of an overall theme. Try to recall what you read the previous day so that you maintain a sense of continuity.

- Spend time thinking about how to apply what God has said to you. Ask Him to help you do this.

- Pray the prayer at the end as if it were your own. Perhaps add your own prayer in response to what you have read and been thinking about.

Join in the conversation on Facebook
facebook.com/jefflucasuk

We are loved as we are

Happy new year! Surely we are all welcoming 2021 with hopes for better times, and that the pandemic is behind us – or soon will be. I am writing these notes in 2020, and while there are shoots of hope, we don't know if a second wave is coming or how bad it will be if it does. We all long for a better season ahead, and we walk into the new year with the God who so often brings change, renewal, newness. But before we begin to consider that in greater depth, let's ponder a truth that is never going to change: the reality that He loves us with a passionate love. As we turn to the prophet Isaiah, addressing a people stranded in exile in Babylon, we see God promise a fresh beginning. But first comes the assurance that they are a people deeply loved by Him.

The truth of God's love for us sits at the very heart of the gospel – God loves His world and everyone in it. Yet that wonderful truth can be diminished because, as Christians, we are so familiar with it. Most of us can quote John 3:16 off by heart, but I've discovered that, because I know it so well, it no longer has the impact on me that it should, and then I drift into trying to earn God's love rather than resting in its security. Maybe you find the same. Before we take one step forward into 2021, let's celebrate that, right now, as we are, we are wonderfully loved. Whatever changes and uncertainties there might be ahead, His love for us will be unwavering. Thank God!

Prayer: Settle my heart to be at peace, secure in the knowledge of Your great love for me, heavenly Father. Amen.

Read:
Isaiah 43:1–4
John 3:1–21

FOCUS

'*Since you are precious and honoured in my sight, and because I love you, I will give people in exchange for you, nations in exchange for your life.*' (Isa. 43:4)

we are
wonderfully
loved

Read:
Isaiah 43:1–5
Matthew 28:16–19

With us in the new

Newness is attractive – I love the smell of leather in a new car, for example, and have even been known to buy the air freshener that simulates that aroma! But change and newness can be intimidating as well. Most of us like the snugness of our comfort zones and while there are some who relish change – and will create it if it's not happening – most of us experience some jitters when we find ourselves in an unfamiliar set of circumstances.

I remember when Kay and I decided to relocate back to the UK from the USA, having spent five years there. With two young children, we only had a temporary place to rent for six months, and very limited income – the promise of around £4,000 per year. Where would we end up living, and how would we cope? I can remember the sinking feeling in my stomach as the plane landed at Heathrow. But we did have a sense that God had called us, and was with us. The promise of His faithful presence is repeatedly affirmed in Scripture – often many questions are 'answered' with this one line response: 'I will be with you.' God never just sends, He accompanies.

To ponder: What difference does it make that God promises always to be with us?

'I will be with you'

Remember and forget

Read:
Isaiah 43:6–18
Jeremiah 16:14–15

FOCUS
'Forget the former things; do not dwell on the past.'
(Isa. 43:18)

Oxymorons are phrases made up of seemingly contradictory words placed together; for example, deafening silence, pretty ugly, and icy hot. In today's reading, God seems to be saying remember and forget. Initially, God is reminding His people of the power that He wielded to deliver their ancestors. The description of God rescuing His people from the chariots of their enemies, leading them through the sea, clearly points them back to the Exodus – the single most defining episode in Israel's history so far. Having called them to remember, however, God then immediately tells them to 'forget the former things'. What? Remember – and forget?

As we consider the God who gives renewal and newness, we realise that recalling our personal histories can be helpful, but we should never be trapped by them. We can become imprisoned in the idea that if God acted in a particular way in the past, He will always use that method. In Israel's case, God was calling His people to stop seeing themselves as being under punishment, and to stop yearning for the glory days when they were powerful. What God had in mind for them was quite different from anything they had experienced.

Let's look back on our journey with the Lord with gratitude, allowing our faith to be strengthened as we do so, but let's not allow what we've experienced in the past to limit what we think God might yet do in the future.

Prayer: May I be strengthened by my history, but never constrained by it, faithful God. Amen.

Newness from God

Read:
Isaiah 43:19–24
Ephesians 6:18–20

FOCUS

'See, I am doing a new thing!'
(Isa. 43:19)

Watching a rerun of a television show from the seventies, I was amazed by the language and attitudes. Some of the humour was blatantly racist, and women were treated with huge disrespect. The comedian seemed to be actively encouraging behaviour that we'd now rightly define as sexual assault. I'm glad we're clearly calling out some of the dysfunctional thinking of the past. But that said, we can fall into the trap of deciding all our beliefs are superior because we live in more modern, enlightened times – C. S. Lewis called this pomposity 'chronological snobbery'. We do live with greater technology and have access to so much information, but that doesn't automatically make us wiser. What is new is not always what is best, and an idea, a method or a way of thinking is not superior simply because it is new.

The Church must be willing to adapt and embrace change, but we want the new thing that *God* is doing – emphasised in these words from Isaiah – rather than quickly latching onto the new just because it *is* new. As we will see tomorrow, that calls for all of us to practise wise discernment, especially those in leadership positions. This is not because they have superior insight, but because they are expected to lead the way. The apostle Paul repeatedly asked for prayer. Pray for church leaders today. Church leadership can be a demanding task, and requires both wisdom and grace.

Prayer: All-wise God, grant wisdom, courage and grace to those who lead Your people. Amen.

Respond with perception

We had not long moved to America, and I found driving on the wrong side of the road (or the right side, depending on your point of view) was an interesting challenge. I was behind the wheel of a church minibus, and didn't realise that I was actually driving on the hard shoulder – not a good idea. I had the cruise control set, and knew that I was moving at the legal speed, so when the police car came up behind me, it didn't occur to me that they wanted to have a little roadside chat.

On came those flashing red and blue lights. I slowed down a little to let the policeman pass. He didn't, but stayed on my tail, and then put his siren on. Now I was being followed by a police car with lights pulsing and siren blaring... but surely I was not the object of interest. Finally the officer decided to yell at me through the public address klaxon on the roof of his car: 'Pull over – right now!' I pulled over, immediately, and then compounded my foolish behaviour by jumping out of the car to talk to the policeman – something you should never do in America. If stopped, stay seated, hands on the wheel. Now I was facing an angry law enforcement official who was pointing the business end of a gun my way. Not good. He had repeatedly been trying to get my attention, and was understandably very frustrated.

When God does something new, we need to respond with perception. And that means turning off spiritual cruise control – be alert, be present.

Prayer: Give me a heart sensitive to Your Spirit, so when the unfamiliar comes, I can perceive Your hand at work. Amen.

Read:
Isaiah 43:19–24
Proverbs 1:1–7

FOCUS

'See, I am doing a new thing! Now it springs up; do you not perceive it?' (Isa. 43:19)

be present

Embracing the new

Read:
Isaiah 43:25
Micah 7:18–19

FOCUS

'I, even I, am he who blots out your transgressions, for my own sake, and remembers your sins no more.'
(Isa. 43:25)

New seasons often begin with God meeting shame-shrouded souls, feeling like abject failures who have no hope. Wearied by their own failed resolutions, they sentence themselves to sameness: 'I'll never change. I can't be any different. Life will just grind on, with me trapped in the same destructive cycle.' And then God comes, and a brand-new horizon opens up. But, as we'll see when we consider some of the characters who experienced these new seasons, shame and guilt have to be dealt with. Regrets about the past need resolution before a new future can even be anticipated.

As God speaks to His people about the stunning new thing He is about to do, He promises to forgive their sin: in fact, to remember it no more. Our sins don't slip His mind; He doesn't say, 'It doesn't matter, it was no big thing.' There's real intentionality here: God discloses His choice to so put aside our sins that He will no longer call them to remembrance. Notice too that He does this 'for my own sake'. What does that mean? When we look elsewhere at Scripture, we discover that the integrity of God's name and character is proven by His willingness to utterly forgive. Ezekiel prophesied, 'You will know that I am the Lord, when I deal with you for my name's sake and not according to your evil ways and your corrupt practices, you people of Israel, declares the Sovereign Lord' (Ezek. 20:44).

Let's accept God's decision to 'remember no more', and choose to live in the freedom and forgiveness He offers.

His willingness to utterly forgive

Prayer: I am humbled by Your grace, Father. Help me live in the good of it today. Amen.

WAVERLEY ABBEY

Transforming lives

Waverley Abbey's vision is to enable people to experience personal transformation through applying God's Word to their lives and relationships.

Our Bible-based training and resources help people around the world to:
• Grow in their walk with God
• Understand and apply Scripture to their lives
• Resource themselves and their church
• Develop pastoral care and counselling skills
• Train for leadership
• Strengthen relationships, marriage and family life and much more.

Our insightful writers provide daily Bible reading notes and engaging resources for everyone, and our experienced course designers and presenters have gained an international reputation for excellence and effectiveness.

Our Waverley Abbey House training and conference centre in Surrey, England, provides excellent facilities in idyllic settings – ideal for both learning and spiritual refreshment.

waverleyabbey.org

New every morning

....

FOCUS

*'Because of the
LORD's great love we
are not consumed,
for his compassions
never fail. They are
new every morning;
great is your
faithfulness.'*
(Lam. 3:22–23)

Our home is in Colorado, but because we still spend quite a lot of time in the UK, speaking at churches, conferences and on radio, we have a flat in southern England, fully equipped with a larder. Often, I will discover what *was* a healthy snack at the back of this cupboard. Closer inspection reveals that it passed its sell-by date ten years ago, and is only fit for the bin. No longer flavourful (and who knows, possibly dangerous to eat), it is now useless. It's completely expired... totally out of date.

As we turn for a moment to the book of Lamentations, a generally bleak book with the destruction of Jerusalem in 586 BC as its backdrop, suddenly we see another promise of newness – this time the pledge that God's steadfast love is renewed every morning. The famous and much-loved hymn *Great is Thy Faithfulnes* is based upon this truth. The singer Beverly Shea (1909–2013), a long-time colleague of evangelist Billy Graham, introduced the hymn to Britain during his rallies there in 1954.

As I stated earlier, God's faithfulness is not just historic, that God *has* loved us in the past. Nor is it futuristic: that God *will* love us when we have attained a measure of greater maturity and holiness. Today, right at this very second, as your eyes pass over this sentence, you and I *are* utterly and totally loved by the Lord. His love never goes out of date. Whatever our circumstances or emotions, this is the truth. Know that truth, and soak it up today.

Prayer: You never change, and Your love never fails, Lord. I worship You. Amen.

Read:
2 Corinthians 5:17
Isaiah 65:17–25

Part of a whole new world

Back at the beginning of the coronavirus pandemic, when many different countries gave a weekly round of applause for medical staff and other frontline workers, I found myself on the edge of tears every time. I was impacted by the sense that I was part of something bigger: a nation standing together in the face of adversity.

Together, we are part of something much bigger than we are as individuals: the Church. As we turn to Paul's famous words to the Corinthian church, reminding them they are new creations in Christ, we discover what God has done is nothing less than create a whole new species of humanity. We will consider what this new creature looks like over the next few days but before we do, let's understand that Paul is saying we are part of a new age, the ultimate renewal of everything, first evidenced in us as believers. We are not just born again as individuals: we are part of a cosmic programme of renewal – something much bigger than us. So let's not say, 'I'm only human', because that is not true – we are newly human, with new power, new purpose, and a new way to live!

To ponder: Do we think enough about what it means to be part of something much greater than ourselves?

we are part of a cosmic programme of renewal

Inclusivity for all

Read:
2 Corinthians 5:17
1 Timothy 1:12–17

FOCUS

'Therefore, if anyone is in Christ, the new creation has come'
(2 Cor. 5:17)

'You don't understand, Jeff. I would love to become a Christian, but I've done too many horrible things. I've hurt too many people. For me to suddenly get religious would be a mockery. It's not for me.'

He turned away, sadness shrouding his face, his shoulders slumped under the weight of his shameful history. But he was wrong. As Paul talks about the new creation, he uses the phrase, 'if anyone is in Christ'. In throwing open the doors of invitation and inclusion to all people everywhere, commentators believe that Paul was musing over the incredible wonder that he himself could be called one of these new-creation people.

When we look over Paul's writings, we realise that while he knew he had received the outrageous grace of God for his past, he never lost his regret for what he had done, or his gratitude and amazement at God's forgiveness. Writing to his young apprentice Timothy, Paul doesn't hesitate to fully own his terrible past actions as a persecutor of the Church. He dubs himself a 'blasphemer and a persecutor and a violent man' (1 Tim. 1:13). Luke paints a graphic, terrible picture of Paul's previous life: 'But Saul began to destroy the church. Going from house to house, he dragged off both men and women and put them in prison' (Acts 8:3). His murderous campaign led to the deaths of some of his victims (Acts 22:4; 26:10). But now, as he says, 'if anyone', we remember that the invitation is for all. For you, for me. Thank God.

Prayer: Your love includes me, Father. Thank God. Amen.

Exclusivity in Jesus

t's been said that searching for God is considered to be cool, but finding Him is not. The quest for understanding and meaning is viewed positively, but if a person comes to clearly understand the revelation of God in Christ, it can be viewed as dogmatic and narrow. As Paul points to Christ as the sole agent of the new creation, however, he shows us the way to God is indeed a narrow path. Jesus alone is the way. According to Jesus, real change comes as a result of the Holy Spirit's activity in our lives, and it is Christ who sends the Holy Spirit. Deep change is only possible through the triune Godhead. This wonderful truth may get us into trouble, and perhaps persecution will come because of it. We won't ruffle any feathers if we proclaim that Jesus is *a* way to new life – that will fit in perfectly with pluralist thinking. But when we insist – because Jesus Himself affirmed – that He is actually *the* way – that's when there will be howls of protest.

To be absolutely clear about anything is perceived by some – perhaps a vocal minority – as intolerant dogmatism. The invitation to all to experience new life will be diluted and ultimately nullified if we do not affirm that Jesus alone offers that renewal because life is uniquely available through Him. This is not the claim of the Church, but the claim of Christ. Let's stand kindly in our faith, without arrogance but having full confidence in it.

Prayer: You are the way, Lord. Help me to live in the strength as well as the challenge of that truth. Amen.

Read:
2 Corinthians 5:17
John 14:6

FOCUS

'Therefore, if anyone is in Christ, the new creation has come' (2 Cor. 5:17)

Let's stand kindly in our faith

New driving force

Read:
**2 Corinthians
5:1–14**
Galatians 2:20

FOCUS

'For Christ's love compels us, because we are convinced that one died for all, and therefore all died.' (2 Cor. 5:14)

Christians are called to be passionate people, committed to Christ whatever the cost. Firm in our convictions, sacrificial in our giving, we want God to use us for His purposes. But passion can be dangerous, especially when it is misguided. In his former life, Paul (then known as Saul) was highly religious, zealous for the law. This passion fuelled his campaign of terror against the Church with devastating results, as we've already seen. But now, a new creature in Christ, he has a new motivation – the love of God, mingled with the knowledge of 'what it is to fear the Lord' (2 Cor. 5:11), which is not a cringing terror, but an attitude of reverence and respect.

Some Christians are driven by love, but love that appears to have very little respect for God's ways. Quoting the famous text, 'Do not judge, or you too will be judged (Matt. 7:1), they refuse to draw any moral conclusions. But we are called by God to be discerning as we weigh up prophecy and call each other to account, so that God's reputation is not tarnished. Jesus brought judgment to the Pharisees, who were guilty of nit-picking and distorting God's message. Others rush to judge, but there is little love, and they seem delighted to point the finger of accusation. New-creation people will be motivated by love, however, and will also be people of integrity because they are principled. Zeal without love will damage. Love without a commitment to what is right can cause damage too. God give us both.

love...
integrity...
God give
us both

Prayer: In standing for and upon truth, may love for You and others be my motivation. Amen.

Waverley Abbey College

'We are all on a journey of discovery when it comes to the matters of the soul, and it is always good to question what we are saying and doing in relation to helping people and their problems.' – Selwyn Hughes, Founder of CWR

Our programmes equip students with the skills and knowledge to release their God-given potential to operate in roles that help people.

Central to all of our teaching is the Waverley Integrative Framework. Built on 50 years of experience, the model emphasises the importance of genuineness, unconditional acceptance and empathy in relationships.

Counselling
As society begins to realise the extent of its brokenness, we continue to recognise the need to train people to support those who are struggling with everyday life, providing training to equip individuals to become professional counsellors. Whatever their starting point in academic learning, we have a pathway to help all students on their academic journey.

Spiritual Formation
For those wanting to be better equipped to help others on their spiritual journey, this programme provides robust and effective Spiritual Formation training. Students engage with theology, psychology, social sciences, historical studies, counselling, leadership studies and psychotherapy.

For more information about all of our course offerings available, visit **waverleyabbeycollege.ac.uk** or come along to a free Open Day.

New servants

Read:
2 Corinthians
5:14–15
Romans 14:7–9

....

FOCUS

'And he died for all, that those who live should no longer live for themselves but for him who died for them and was raised again.'
(2 Cor. 5:15)

I didn't really understand this question when it was first put to me, the night I became a Christian: 'Would you like to give your life to Christ?' It was so easily posed, and yet it had massive implications. My life was much simpler back then – no mortgage to pay, no long-term commitments to shoulder, no wife or family to care for. Without too much thought or reflection, I 'gave my life' to Jesus. In a way, it would have been better for me to have thought a bit longer and harder about such a totally revolutionary choice that would transform my life. In a story about a building project, we hear of the vital importance of counting the cost of our choices (Luke 14:25–35). As it turned out, I only gradually learned what was involved in giving my life. It is an ongoing process: I am still figuring out the implications of that moment that occurred decades ago. I am glad, however, that I made that decision. Whenever I think about what a new creature in Christ looks like, I find myself recalling that old decision, and renewing it.

Paul teaches us that a Christian characteristic is that we no longer live for ourselves, but for Christ. Dietrich Bonhoeffer warned against the dangers of what he called 'cheap grace': believing in the value and significance of the death of Christ, but not moved to make much response to it. Living for Jesus – giving Him our lives – is surely a daily choice. Let's choose well today.

Prayer: I thoughtfully, deliberately, give You myself this day, Father. My life is Yours. Spend me. Amen.

Living for
Jesus... a
daily choice

A new view of Jesus

Read:
2 Corinthians 5:16
Acts 9:1–9

I t seems odd but Paul, previously Saul, probably knew of Jesus during His earthly ministry. Jesus caused quite a stir in Jerusalem, especially in the last year of His public ministry, when He made a significant impact during the feasts of Tabernacles, Dedication, and Passover. Commentators believe that Saul would have been very aware of the man Jesus. As he began his awful persecution of the Church, condemning followers of Jesus to death, he must have already taken the view that Jesus Himself was a blasphemous fraud. When Saul had that life-altering encounter with the risen, ascended Jesus on the Damascus Road, he heard Christ ask the question, 'Why do you persecute me?' Not only was Jesus fully identifying Himself with His people – when they suffer, He suffers with them – but He was also pointing out that Saul's horrible campaign was personal, directed at Him.

FOCUS

'So from now on we regard no one from a worldly point of view. Though we once regarded Christ in this way, we do so no longer.' (2 Cor. 5:16)

But now Saul's view of Jesus had radically changed in a moment. Jesus was not a blaspheming man who deserved to die. Instead, He really was the Son of God, the One who now had the right to take charge of Saul's life. Christ was now the foundation, the focus, the centre of Saul's existence.

It's possible to slide into a Christ-less Christian life. We maintain Christian ethics, continue in Christian habits like church going, but our connection with Jesus fades. For Paul, walking by faith with the living Christ was his priority. May it be ours too.

Prayer: I want to know You, Lord, and Your living, active, transforming, personal presence. Amen.

A new way to look at others

Paul's encounter with Jesus also transformed how he viewed others. Once a separatist Jew who saw Gentiles as 'dogs', now he viewed Gentile believers as Abraham's offspring, brothers and sisters in Christ (Gal. 3:26–29; Eph. 2:11–19). Radically departing from his previous thinking, now he saw Jewish unbelievers as in need of Christ's salvation (Rom. 10:1–4). And there are a number of times when Paul describes others as those for whom Christ died (see 1 Cor. 8:11). If we have truly 'seen' Jesus for who He really is, then that must affect our relationships with each other. In his epistle, John the beloved repeatedly tells us loving God and loving others are intertwined.

Sadly, we can easily label people according to our prejudices. And prejudice causes us to notice and amplify that which confirms our conclusions about them, and edit out that which contradicts those conclusions. We may think we are open-minded, but we can be heavily blinkered, and need to challenge ourselves.

May God help us to see people for who they really are, and not as we have judged them to be.

To ponder: When have you become aware of your own prejudice?

loving God and loving
others are intertwined

The Spirit renews

It's a common misunderstanding about faith. It's assumed Christians are simply people with a belief system that motivates them to behave in a Christian way – following the rules because they believe in God. But that's not true. As we've seen, Christians are new creations, daily engaging with the supernatural – with the power of the Holy Spirit, who is the agent of inner transformation. Our minds are being renewed, and that activity of God in our thinking brings change in the way we behave. This inward change is the work of the Holy Spirit (Titus 3:5), who gradually transforms believers into the image of Christ, 'with ever-increasing glory' (2 Cor. 3:18). Our inner being is renewed daily, by the Spirit's power.

Do we have any part in all of this, or is it solely God's action and responsibility? As Paul tells his friends in Ephesus to 'put on the new self', he calls them to co-operate with God in that process. His power is at work, but we still need to choose to obey, and to make our response to God a priority. We are told to 'seek first' God's kingdom. Paul reminds the church in Galatia, where people were arguing about the external ritual of circumcision, that being part of this new creation God is bringing to pass is all that really matters (Gal. 6:15). We'll revisit this later, but for now let's know that our choices matter, and submission to God and intentional obedience are vital if we are to experience true change.

Read:
Ephesians 4:17–24
Colossians 3:1–11

FOCUS

'put on the new self, created to be like God in true righteousness and holiness' (Eph. 4:24)

Prayer: I'm grateful that You call me to partner with You in the shaping of my life, Father. May I do that today. Amen.

New habits

Read:
Colossians 3:1–17
Romans 6:1–4

....

FOCUS

'Do not lie to each other, since you have taken off your old self with its practices and have put on the new self, which is being renewed in knowledge in the image of its Creator.'
(Col. 3:9–10).

I used to swear a lot before I became a Christian. I swore in a rather creative way, which often made people laugh, which is probably why I did it. I also used to tell lies. I remember telling my family a few whoppers about projects we were doing in woodwork at school. Thankfully, they never wondered out loud why I didn't bring some of those mythical masterpieces home. As a new Christian, I quickly learned that using bad language was not acceptable in our youth group, and lying was frowned upon too. Slowly, the habits were broken.

Paul talks again about the new life that is in Christ – one no longer characterised by 'filthy language' (Col. 3:8) and lying (or anger, rage, malice and slander). As he does so, he uses imagery that would have reminded the Colossians of their baptism in water, where they removed some (some say all) of their clothing before being immersed, and then put on new, fresh clothes afterwards. He also stresses that racism has no place in the new creation community, because now we are all one in Christ Jesus, so our attitudes to others may need to change. Paul reminds the Roman Christians that grace is not made available to give us a free pass to sin, but rather empowers us to live in the newness of life. A life truly given to Christ will not only experience initial change following conversion, but ongoing change – consecration. Are we living the new life, or slipping back into the habits of the old?

we are all one in Christ Jesus

Prayer: Enable me to live in such a way that speaks of Your purity, goodness and holiness, loving Father. Amen.

God's Plan for your Wellbeing

NEW book and Church Programme

Journey with Dave Smith through this 50-day
devotional and the the story of the prophet
Elijah, as you explore God's plan for your
wellbeing. Dave also shares some of the
lesson's he has learnt in order to help you,
your Church, or your small group achieve the
physical, emotional and spiritual balance that
enables you to flourish for God and for good.

GOD'S PLAN FOR YOUR
Wellbeing

50-DAY GUIDE
DAVE SMITH

Find out more at
waverleyabbeyresources.org/GPFYW

God's renewing work

Read:
2 Corinthians
4:1–18
2 Corinthians 3:18

FOCUS

'Though outwardly we are wasting away, yet inwardly we are being renewed day by day.'
(2 Cor. 4:16)

It's a slogan sometimes used by Christians: 'Be patient with me: God hasn't finished with me yet.' And it is true. Having looked at how God is the God of renewal and freshness, tomorrow we will begin to look at some people who were blessed with new beginnings. But before we do, we should realise God's renewing work is happening daily. It isn't reserved for crisis moments, when a voice from above suddenly speaks to us. It is, instead, a daily, ongoing work of the Holy Spirit in each one of us as children of God.

Notice, however, that this renewing work is not always obvious. It is a gradual lifelong project. Frankly, as I look back over 40 years of following Christ, I know that I have grown in Him, but I have not changed for the better nearly as much as I anticipated when I set out on this journey. Perhaps you feel the same about yourself. While it may be that we are more aware of our faults than our positive characteristics, any progress can seem very slow. As Paul writes about inner transformation, and living in a new age of the Spirit, we recognise that we experience this by faith. Our bodies age and fade, showing us the transient nature of this life, but we are being shaped and prepared for living fully in the age to come. To put it bluntly, as Paul does, we're wasting away, but being renewed too!

God's renewing work is happening daily

Prayer: When I am frustrated with myself, help me to put my hope in You and Your power to form me into the image of Christ. Amen.

Religious people can be dangerous

Read:
John 8:1–3
Luke 4:28–30

FOCUS

'The teachers of the law and the Pharisees brought in a woman caught in adultery.' (John 8:3)

This story is not mentioned in the earliest manuscripts but it is entirely consistent with the tone of the Gospels and worthy of consideration. It shows a traumatised woman dragged through the streets and dumped in front of a hostile crowd. I can't imagine how she felt, faced with such derision. Some say that a stoning was unlikely because the Roman authorities would have disapproved. They were the agents of justice at this point in Israel's history. Nevertheless, she must have been terrified. Mob violence could have broken out as it did when Jesus caused offence while preaching in His home town of Nazareth, and the crowd tried to throw Him off a cliff. Religious incitement and crowds can create unpredictable behaviour.

Those gathered were keen to punish her, but some commentators draw attention to the maxim, 'No penalty without a warning', which meant you had to be warned before you could be condemned. It was the religious barons who were treating her so roughly, the teachers of the law, who should have known better. Religious people can be very dangerous, armed with their interpretation of Scripture. Even though, as we'll consider later, this trap was really being set for Jesus, they were also using the law to justify their heartless behaviour. The Word of God is like a sword. Let's not swing it around thoughtlessly, because when we do, people get hurt.

Prayer: Lord Jesus, in standing for truth, may I never lose sight of people. Amen.

Objectified and shamed

Read:
John 8:1–4
1 Timothy 5:17–20

FOCUS

'They made her stand before the group' (John 8:3)

Looking back over four decades of ministry in general and local church leadership in particular, I regret a few episodes, and wish I could undo them. One of them involved a volunteer in our church who had messed up. While not on our full-time team, he was respected as a leader and influencer. When what he'd done wrong – a one-off event, quite out of character – was discovered, we took the view that he should be removed from leadership and the entire church membership told about his transgression. What we did not only shamed him, but brought embarrassment to his wife and children as well. We justified our actions by taking a superficial view of church discipline, and the verse we quoted was 'those who sin rebuke before all.' We did not take into account the thought that the public rebuke was intended for those influencers who had brought scandal upon the Early Church. They would have been rebuked privately first, and only publicly if they refused to repent after that. Our well-intentioned shaming was unnecessary.

The woman brought before Jesus was made to stand before the crowd of men, some of whom may even have been leering, voyeurs enjoying the news that she had been caught in the very act of adultery. Commentators note she could have been held in custody while the case was discussed with Jesus. There is a place for church discipline, as the Bible makes clear. But when that happens, may it be done with great wisdom and care.

Prayer: When discipline is needed in Your Church, may love not be a casualty, merciful God. Amen.

Read:
John 8:1–6
Matthew 22:15–22

Set up in a trap

At times, after I have preached at a church, someone will approach me with a question, during the after-church nattering. The conversation tends to begin with 'During your message tonight, you mentioned this point about God/this view of the Second Coming/an approach to the Sabbath, *but…*' and then comes the question.

I have no problems with questions: they are one sign a church is healthy, and not a cult. Sometimes, however, the questioner isn't looking for an answer. They just want to argue for the sake of it, on their pet subject, or perhaps to edge me into an awkward situation.

The leaders here were laying a trap for Jesus – the text is emphatic about that. If Jesus agreed to an execution, He would be encouraging them to break Roman law, which did not provide for a death penalty in such cases. If he discouraged the stoning, He could be charged with offending against the law of God. The question was a loaded one. Either answer would involve Jesus in difficulties, which, of course, was the aim of the exercise. When we disagree, let's check our motives.

To ponder: Why do some people want to win an argument rather than find understanding?

When we disagree, let's check our motives

Hypocrisy

Read:
John 8:1–6
Matthew 23:13–39

FOCUS

'In the Law Moses commanded us to stone such women.'
(John 8:5)

People of faith are sometimes accused of being hypocrites and, in some cases, the charge is justified. There are some who preach one kind of behaviour, while living an entirely different life. But there is a difference between hypocrisy and human fragility. We Christians do not (or should not) suggest we are perfect, or that we've arrived in our life journey. On the contrary, we need to regularly acknowledge that we are in need of God's salvation, unable to help ourselves. Only God can change our hearts and lives.

Sadly, these religious barons were guilty of rank hypocrisy and, as we've seen, their sickening behaviour could have led to a woman losing her life rather than beginning a new one. They twisted words of Scripture around as they said, 'such women', whereas both relevant passages (Lev. 20:10; Deut. 22:22) say that the man as well as the woman was to be put to death. Where was the man in this situation? Clearly, it takes two to commit adultery. And then these religious leaders were proposing a lynching, not a punishment that followed a trial – no trial is suggested. In calling for justice, they were blatantly ignoring basic principles of justice. This was hypocrisy. During the coronavirus pandemic, the public were outraged when political leaders created rules that they themselves flouted. Let's never insist that others live by principles that we ignore.

Prayer: Save me from hypocrisy, Lord. Flawed as I am, I want to live authentically for You. Amen.

live
authentically

Sex and sexism

Read:
John 8:1–6
Ephesians 5:1–20

FOCUS

'In the Law Moses commanded us to stone such women.' (John 8:5)

It's a problem that the Church has wrestled with throughout history. When someone messes up sexually, the response is usually swifter and stronger than when other patterns of negative behaviour are revealed. Church communities tend to react more readily to such problems, but can ignore or lessen their response when the issue is greed, gossip or envy. It's interesting that these religious leaders chose sex as the sin in presenting this 'test case' to Jesus.

There's blatant sexism in this episode too, because, as we've already seen, the accused in this story is a woman. No man is indicted. Judaism in Jesus' time had a negative view of women, viewing them generally as the likely instigators whenever sexual sin was committed. Women were seen as lacking sufficient character and moral fibre to deal with sexual temptation; the hormonal struggles of adolescent boys were blamed on girls. A woman who committed sexual sin was marked, but men were not.

Perhaps there is still a hint of this in our culture: the fictional James Bond can be seen as a man's man, as he beds a variety of attractive females, but women who behave the same way are seen as loose. Though the so-called sexual revolution has perhaps changed things, our sexual morality is important. We are called to live distinctive lives of purity and integrity. That is true of all, regardless of gender. But God wants to bring whole-life change, which includes, but is not limited to, our sexual ethics.

Prayer: Work in every area of my life, Holy Spirit, that I might bring glory to Christ. Amen.

Scribbling and silence

Read:
John 8:1–8
Haggai 1:5–7

FOCUS

'But Jesus bent down and started to write on the ground with his finger' (John 8:6)

Imagine the scene with me. You are badgering Jesus with a question, impatiently waiting for His response – perhaps with much foot-tapping, huffing and puffing. You have others with you to back you up, and they, too, are standing there, hands on hips, insistent on a reply. He says nothing, but just starts writing with His finger in the sand. We don't know what He wrote, and speculation has been endless. Some say that Jesus scribbled the words of Jeremiah 17:13: 'Those who turn away from you will be written in the dust because they have forsaken the LORD, the spring of living water'. Others suggest that in the two separate writing incidents, Jesus first scribbled 'Do not help a guilty person by being a malicious witness' (Exod. 23:1), and the second time, 'Have nothing to do with a false charge and do not put an innocent or honest person to death, for I will not acquit the guilty' (Exod. 23:7). And then others suggest that Jesus was writing a list of the sins of the accusers!

While we can speculate, we just don't know what was written that day. Even though He was giving them a moment to pause, they didn't take it, they didn't let up and they didn't relax the pressure He was under. Perhaps Jesus was simply giving them a little time to consider their own hearts, to see what they had become, but they didn't take it. Finally, He confronts them with words rather than scribbling. When all is quiet, let's face ourselves, and then change can come.

let's face ourselves, and then change can come

Prayer: Lord, help me to take time to quietly consider my ways. Amen.

A great question

After 42 years of marriage, there is much that I have learned about my ever-loving (and sometimes ever-forbearing) wife, Kay. I know that she doesn't like surprises, loves chocolate, and the sound of her grandsons' laughter is the sweetest music to her ears. And I also know that if I addressed her as 'woman', it would not go down well. It sounds cold, clinical and, frankly, disrespectful, and as we hear Jesus addressing the terrified accused lady, His language does seem sterile. But we're wrong, because in His culture, this address was perfectly acceptable – Jesus spoke to His own mother in those terms on two occasions.

What followed is rather beautiful because He asks the question, 'Who condemns you?' Press 'Pause' for a moment because the discussion with the elders had centred around her sin and the appropriate punishment for it. But Jesus' response is surprising because He doesn't ask, 'Did you do it?' In fact, His next statement, which we'll consider tomorrow, presupposes that she did. Instead, His comment was about the lack of condemnation rather than her sin. And in saying, 'Then neither do I condemn you', Jesus is assuming the position that only God can assume – the ability to respond to human sin. He doesn't mention forgiveness, just an absence of condemnation. We don't pretend to be faultless – John the beloved shows us the futility and self-deception of that – but thank God, we have a Saviour, not an accuser.

Read:
John 8:9–10
1 John 1:8–10

FOCUS

'Jesus straightened up and asked her, "Woman, where are they? Has no one condemned you?"' (John 8:10)

Prayer: I am so grateful, Lord, for Your mercy and grace. I stand confident on the firm foundation of Your love. Amen.

Giving hope

It is our desire to see daily bible reading notes used more widely, to see Christians grow in their relationship with Jesus on a daily basis and to see Him reflected in their everyday living.

More than 60,000 copies each year are delivered into prisons too and our vision is to grow this ministry even further, putting these notes into the hands of those in challenging situations and to see their lives transformed through a new and growing relationship with Jesus.

David, an ex-prisoner said "Thank you so much for your generous gift of Every Day With Jesus. Whilst in prison each issue spoke to me where I was emotionally and mentally at the time. Each copy helped me to feel loved, despite all my sin and rejection. It's not that I've never been loved, I've just never allowed myself to feel it. Now love has filled me up and overflows out of me. I thank God for your work, because, by your work, gifted from God, you've helped another sinner for which I'll be eternally grateful".

Every Day with Jesus

Clearly there are costs to provide this ministry and we are trusting in God's provision.

Could you be part of this vision? Do you have the desire to see lives transformed through a relationship with Jesus?

A small donation from you of just £2 a month, by direct debit, will make such a difference. Giving hope to someone in desperate need whilst you too grow deeper in your own relationship with Jesus.

Go and sin no more

Read:
John 8:1–11
Romans 6:1–4

FOCUS

'Then neither do I condemn you,' Jesus declared. 'Go now and leave your life of sin.' (John 8:11)

A few days ago we saw that the earliest manuscripts don't have the story of the woman caught in adultery. That said, most scholars argue for its inclusion because it's entirely consistent with the core message of the gospel. But one or two of the scholars that I refer to ignore the story altogether. Is that because they fear the possibility of the story being misunderstood, as if Jesus is being light on sin, especially sexual sin? As we have seen already, it was Dietrich Bonhoeffer who coined the term 'cheap grace'. Bonhoeffer was concerned that grace could be twisted into a free pass for ongoing patterns of sinfulness; forgiveness without discipleship. But that's not what is happening here.

As we saw yesterday, Jesus speaks those beautiful words, 'Then neither do I condemn you'. He doesn't refer to her adultery specifically: there is no need to shame her further. But He doesn't stop there. He charges the woman to leave her life of sin. This is not to suggest she was a prostitute or in the habit of adultery, just a broad statement about sinful living. This was a call to make a clean break from her previous lifestyle and embrace a new start. Jesus did not treat sin lightly; when He encountered people in destructive lifestyles, He offered them the opportunity to live life differently – a new life. Or as one writer put it so succinctly, 'Mercy from God calls for life unto God'.*

Have we been forgiven, only to keep returning to that old way of life?

Prayer: I never want to use grace as a permit to sinful patterns of behaviour, Father. Fill me with Your Spirit. Amen.

*George R. Beasley-Murray, *John: Word Biblical Commentary* (Zondervan: Grand Rapids, MI, USA, 2012)p147

New life and believing

I'd travelled hundreds of miles to speak at an event arranged by a group of local churches, and now my heart was heavy. Hundreds had been expected, but appalling weather meant that few had braved the downpour, and just a few dozen hardy souls sat shivering in the pews. The organiser was doing his best to be positive and put on a brave face. 'Don't worry, Jeff. We are still believing for a last-minute rush.' And that sparked a question in my soul: what does it mean to believe? Were those words – 'We are still believing' – an act of faith? And if not, what were they?

Believing is a common and vital Bible word. In writing his Gospel, John sets out his purpose, calling people to a belief that will lead to new life. Belief is not just about being hopeful, or saying that you think something will happen. As we'll see, it's tenacious faith in the power and goodness of God, regardless of circumstances. It's about trust when what we want doesn't happen. And it's about refusing to succumb to the grip of fear. Today, may the Lord increase our faith.

To ponder: This episode is about two battles between fear and faith. Have you walked through a similar battle? What did you learn?

Belief is... tenacious faith the power and goodness of God

Facing reality

Read:
Mark 5:21–23
Romans 4:18–25

FOCUS

'He pleaded earnestly with him, "My little daughter is dying."' (Mark 5:23)

The man sidled up to me, a guilty look on his face, apparently nervous that he might be overheard. 'Can I ask you a question?' he whispered, looking this way and that. I urged him to go ahead. So softly that I could barely hear him, he asked, 'Is it all right to say that I have a headache?' I responded by asking, if he had a headache, then why wouldn't he be able to admit it? But he came from a 'health and wealth' church where people were encouraged to 'confess' that they were well while sick because healing would come as they spoke positive words. Not only is this physically dangerous, but surely it leads to all kinds of wider unreality. Jairus was blunt and urgent in his request: 'My little daughter is dying.' The diagnosis was shared with sharp clarity. In fact, his words, literally translated, are faltering, and express his own brokenness and helplessness: 'My daughter... dying... come.'

Abraham had to face the fact that fatherhood at his and Sarah's great ages was impossible. But by faith, he stared down the impossible. Rick Warren, who has known great success and incredible heartache, says, 'Faith is not denying reality. Faith is facing reality without being discouraged by it.'

Surely a new, better chapter in our lives often begins with us facing reality about where we are today. At an AA meeting, anyone battling against alcohol addiction introduces themselves by name, and then adds, 'and I am an alcoholic.' Face reality. Face it with faith.

Prayer: Heavenly Father, when the reality of my situation is overwhelming, help me to face it, with You. Amen.

God is trustworthy, but not predictable

Read:
Mark 5:21–23
Matthew 8:5–13

FOCUS

'My little daughter is dying. Please come and put your hands on her so that she will be healed and live.' (Mark 5:23)

Having been a Christian for quite some time, I can be tempted to think that I have got God figured out – I know how He works, what He'll do. Even as I write those last sentences, the notion seems obviously ridiculous. God is not impetuous, He is utterly trustworthy – but He is not predictable, and does not always work in the same way. When a centurion came to Jesus, he insisted that he was not worthy to have Jesus in his home – but healing came anyway, with Jesus simply speaking the word. Jairus wants Jesus in his home – the method to bring change and healing is different, but the power is the same. I'm nervous of those books that make faith into a formula: *Ten steps to answered prayer*, *Five pathways to power*, and the like. God is not a vending machine.

When we limit God, we risk frustrating His purposes. For the Early Church in Jerusalem, the thought that God would want them to reach the Gentile population was just unthinkable. For one thing, they expected that Jesus would return to Jerusalem and set up a kingdom there. So Jews from around the ancient world would gather, they would not be sent out to reach them. And then the idea of Gentiles being included in the covenant made no sense. So for over a decade – that's a long time – the Gentiles went unreached, until God began to move through those scattered by persecution. How might our preconceived ideas limit the work of God?

Prayer: You are trustworthy, faithful to Your word, unpredictable. Surprise me, expand my view of You, mighty God. Amen.

God is not a vending machine

The absurdity of prayer

Read:
Mark 5:21–23
Hebrews 4:14–16

FOCUS

'My little daughter is dying. Please come and put your hands on her so that she will be healed and live.' (Mark 5:23)

Picture the scene. Jesus is surrounded by crowds of people, frantic hurting souls desperate for help. They press in on Him. But this one man, a respected and influential synagogue leader, asks, 'Please come and help my daughter.' Effectively, Jairus was saying, 'Come away from the crowd, please, and give your attention fully to my sick daughter.' He was passionate in his request. The Greek word used means 'pleading earnestly, begging'. It's the same word used in the story of the Prodigal Son, when the father figure pleads with the elder brother. At first glance, Jairus' pleading seems a little selfish, unless of course it was your daughter who was dying.

Again, these notes are being completed during the dreadful Covid pandemic. Daily we have been bombarded by news of more sickness and death. And so my prayers for wisdom in leadership, for help as I study for next week's sermon, and even for protection for my own family – can seem paltry and even self-centred. But as we'll see, surrounded by need, Jesus responded to Jairus' request.

Prayer always seems a little absurd. You talk to someone you can't see, most often with no direct response back, about the details of your life, while aware that millions of others are also making requests about far more significant issues. Yet prayer is the way that God chooses to do His work of change and intervention. So let's keep praying, asking and believing.

let's keep praying, asking and believing

Prayer: Thank You that I can share my life with You in prayer, Lord. May I do so freely. Amen.

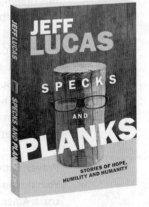

Telling Jesus off

Read:
Mark 5:25–32
Matthew 16:21–23

FOCUS

"'You see the people crowding against you," his disciples answered, "and yet you can ask, 'Who touched me?'"'
(Mark 5:31)

Out on a family horse-riding expedition (one that I wasn't keen on, since horses have no brakes or steering wheels), our daughter Kelly was thrown off when her horse was startled by a snake. I remember the sense of powerlessness that I felt as I knelt beside her, her wounded face gushing blood. There was a source of comfort, however, because in our group was a family doctor, immediately able to assess her injuries. Getting her to the hospital was agony, both for her, physically, and for me, emotionally, because I just wanted her injuries to be attended to, right now. Any delay was awful.

Having convinced Jesus that He should go to his home, Jairus must have been dismayed when Jesus stopped to engage with the woman with the issue of blood. But Jairus was silent, perhaps instinctively aware that, despite his position as a leader in local society, he couldn't order Jesus around. Ironically, the only people who show any frustration in this episode are the disciples, bemused and even irritated by Jesus' questioning about who touched Him. That seemed foolish to them, and they said so. When Jesus later announced He was heading to Jerusalem, to death and resurrection, Peter objected, rebuked Jesus – and got a stinging reply.

God is God. Sometimes, I don't like His methods or His timing. Perhaps you've experienced that frustration too. Jesus brought change as Jairus was patient. Let's follow the synagogue leader's example.

Prayer: Father, when what You do frustrates me, when Your timing seems wrong, help me to submit, to wait, to trust. Amen.

God is God

Imperfect faith

She was in dire straits, struggling at her wits' end. We don't have all the details of her medical condition; we only know her symptom was continual bleeding. Mark is very sharp in his criticism of the doctors – the poor woman had spent all she had in consulting them, without relief. Luke is not so blunt in his description 'but no one could heal her' (Luke 8:43). He's a doctor! Some of the dubious 'cures' of the day included placing gum and crocus in wine, or eating three boiled Persian onions, or standing at a junction of two roads with a cup of wine in your right hand, and then allowing or asking someone to come up behind you and frighten you. Carrying barley corn grown from the dung of a white female donkey was another suggested remedy.

Now, she pushes through the crowd, which was a brave act because her condition made her ritually unclean (Lev. 15:25–30). As she reaches to touch the hem of Jesus' garment, her faith is laced with superstition and even belief in magic. She was following the popular notion that to touch the garment of a powerful person would connect her to supernatural power. Kent Hughes says, 'Her faith was uninformed, presumptuous, and superstitious, but it was real, and Christ honoured her imperfect faith.'* Some say that her faith was selfish because she wanted healing rather than the healer. Faith is always imperfect, but, as we'll see, God knows that and it doesn't put Him off. He still responds.

Read:
Mark 5:25–32
Mark 6:56

FOCUS

'When she heard about Jesus, she came up behind him in the crowd and touched his cloak, because she thought, "If I just touch his clothes, I will be healed."'
(Mark 5:27–28)

Prayer: Lord, I believe. Help my unbelief. Amen.

*R. Kent Hughes, *Mark: Jesus, Servant and Savior*, Vol 1 (Westchester, IL, USA: Crossway Books, 1989) p128

New inclusion

Many of us Christians have no problem believing that God loves the world, but struggle to accept that God loves *us* and wants us to be part of His purposes. Perhaps that's because we know ourselves all too well. Familiar with our temptations, failures and flaws, we quietly wonder if we too could be included. It's like a spiritual form of Imposter Syndrome – if people knew what we are really like, they wouldn't like us, and seeing as God knows exactly what we're like, He probably doesn't like us either.

As Jesus goes to great lengths to discover who it was that had touched Him (the Greek means, 'He kept looking'), we can feel some sympathy for this woman. But He pointed her out in a way that was the opposite of the treatment the religious barons gave to the woman caught in adultery – they exposed her publicly to shame her, whereas Jesus identified this woman to include her. Her condition meant that she had lived as a social pariah. But now, in allowing her to touch His clothing without rebuke – more on that tomorrow – He is bringing her out of the shadows of shame.

To ponder: Do you ever experience spiritual 'Imposter Syndrome'?

out of the shadows of shame

Fearful of Jesus

FOCUS

'Then the woman, knowing what had happened to her, came and fell at his feet and, trembling with fear, told him the whole truth.'
(Mark 5:33)

Imagine how you might feel. You've crept up behind someone, wanting something from them, taking it without asking. You hope to get what you've come for, and then quietly disappear into the crowd. But then your plan collapses, you're discovered and, worse still, exposed before everyone. And that someone is Jesus, and you know He has incredible supernatural power – your instantly healed body says so. You're very afraid, and perhaps for good reason.

It might be that this woman's fear came because she knew that, according to Jewish purity regulations, she had made Jesus unclean by touching His garment. Perhaps she was anxious that she had passed on an infection with that touch, or stolen some of His power – remember all the superstition that was around, with those ridiculous 'cures'. But instead of rebuke, Jesus calls her a daughter. This is stunning. Apart from one example (Mark 2:5), up until this point Jesus had not called anyone – not even His disciples – family members. She expects a rebuke, but she gets healing, peace, blessing.

It's strange to say it, but some of us live nervously around Jesus. In our heart of hearts, we anticipate a telling off rather than a word of encouragement. But the One who wants to work in our lives to bring newness and change comes to us with love and acceptance. We're invited to draw near to God with confidence. Let's not shrink back, because the price for our full access to the Lord has been paid in full.

Prayer: Boldly, gladly, freely, confidently, Lord, I come to You. Amen.

Keep believing

Read:
Mark 5:35–36
Psalm 83:1–18

FOCUS

'Overhearing what they said, Jesus told him, "Don't be afraid; just believe."' (Mark 5:36).

It's surely the most devastating news possible. 'Your child is dead.' For Jairus, the blunt announcement from a group arriving from his home must have been like a dagger to his heart, not least because his hopes had been raised. Not only had Jairus managed to convince Jesus to come to the house and intervene, but he had just witnessed the healing of that woman with the issue of blood. But now, for him, his daughter and family, it was all over, hope dashed into a thousand pieces. Jesus doesn't enter into discussion with the group that brought the tragic news, however: the wording used here suggests that He overheard the comment but dismissed it. Nor does He tell Jairus what the outcome of the day will be, that his daughter will be well. He just exhorts the grieving father to resist fear and believe. The present tense of the Greek word means to 'keep believing', to hold on to faith rather than give in to despair. Faith is not a one-off act, but a daily choice, through the changing seasons of life.

Sometimes I wish God would tell me more, fill in more details about what I should do. But we don't walk by faith because we have all the information; often, we walk without it. And when others suffer, we risk doing them great harm with our well-intentioned tendency to try to fill in the blanks that God has not filled in. Faith is not just about responding to God's voice, but also trusting when He is silent about what He is doing or will do.

Prayer: 'O God, do not remain silent; do not turn a deaf ear, do not stand aloof, O God' (Psa. 83:1). Amen.

New possibilities seem laughable

It was my first day working in a bank in London. I was nervous, wondering if I would be up to the job (and actually I was rather useless as a banker – it's possible that my contribution to the world of finance led to later economic downturns!). But my jitters were compounded because, as a relatively new Christian, I wanted to make an impact for Jesus. My methods weren't particularly subtle – I carried a very large Bible into the lunch room and quietly opened it to read. Across the room, a loud, Jack-the-lad chap broke the silence with an awfully loud enquiry – 'What's that you're reading, then?' Informing him that it was the Bible, he sneered in response. From then on, some people in the bank changed my name from Jeff to God – when I made a mistake, which was often, the word would go out: 'God has made a mistake in his cashbook again.' More laughter.

Greeted by some wailing mourners as He arrived at the synagogue leader's house, Jesus announced the little girl was not dead, just asleep. Mourning customs among the Jews included flute players and people wailing and tearing at their hair and clothes. Even the poorest person had to hire at least one mourner and two flute players – expense added to grief. Jesus was not suggesting that the girl was just in a coma, but rather that, to Him, raising her from the dead was just like waking her from a night's sleep. And they laughed. But He – and Jairus' family – were to have the last laugh.

Prayer: When new possibilities seem laughable, or when others mock me for my faith, help me to stand strong in You, Mighty God. Amen.

Read:
Mark 5:37–40
Luke 23:36–37

....

FOCUS
'But they laughed at him.' (Mark 5:40)

make an
impact
for Jesus

Visit the Holy Land and Jordan 9-17th November 2021

Join Jeff and Kay Lucas on a life changing tour of Israel and Jordan, visiting famous sites that will transform the way you read and view the Bible, including Galilee, Jerusalem and Magdala, the home of Mary Magdalene. Capernaum and the Garden of Gethsemane are included, as well as the amazing desert landscape of Wadi Rum with its idyllic orange sands and rock formations.

Imagine sharing communion while sailing on the Sea of Galilee; exploring the ruins of Capernaum, where Jesus based his ministry; ascending Mount Nebo where Moses viewed the promised land, and sharing worship, prayer and teaching on the beach where Jesus cooked His disciples breakfast after a long night's fishing. And then there's Petra, the world famous archaeological site in Jordan's southwestern desert. Dating to around 300 B.C., it was the capital of the Nabatean Kingdom. Accessed via a narrow canyon called Al Siq, it contains tombs and temples carved into pink sandstone cliffs. Perhaps its most famous structure is 45m-high Al Khazneh, a temple with an ornate, Greek-style facade, and known as the Treasury.

Professional local guides share their wealth of historical and archeological knowledge; Jeff offers teaching as we tour, and Jeff and Kay host the entire experience - one that some travelers have enjoyed so much they have returned to do the same trip a second time!

With excellent hotels, amazing food, and the unforgettable experience of exploring the stunning old city of Jerusalem (with markets where you can haggle for a bargain) this trip will delight and inspire. Come with us!

What others had to say about the tour...

'The memories of this tour are priceless. Jeff brings to life the Bible stories in such a way that one can imagine being there in Bible times.'

'Jeff and Kay kept the momentum of the tour consistent, and the amount of places visited in a very safe and organised fashion is truly remarkable – superb!'

'Our Israel trip was both a spiritual journey and an amazing adventure. Jeff and Kay were great hosts. Our tour guides in Israel and Jordan were knowledgeable and fun.'

'The tour schedule was very manageable and allowed for people to see all the sites, wander alone or just rest. Unforgettable holiday!'

Book your place now and join Jeff and Kay from 9–17 November 2021.

The health and safety of our group members is our number one priority. Our experienced travel agents closely monitor the fast-moving coronavirus situation and are pleased that travel restrictions are being lifted or mitigated in many countries. Our tours strictly adhere to the UK Foreign Office travel advice together with the Israeli Government safety guidelines to ensure all tours operate and conform to any regulations that may be required.

For more information, visit **toursforchristians.com**

Newness and friendship

Read:
Luke 8:51–54
Proverbs 17:17

FOCUS

'When he arrived at the house of Jairus, he did not let anyone go in with him except Peter, John and James, and the child's father and mother.' (Luke 8:51)

Just recently I've been stocktaking, considering who my friends are, and where we are in our relationship together. This may seem rather clinical, but I even drew a chart to show who is in my inner circle, and those who are close but drawing closer. I then thought about those who are closer but moving away from me for whatever reason, where I need to invest – and where I need to let friendships fade. Some were largely centred around function, and now the function has gone, so they no longer operate. If all this sounds strange, let me suggest that Jesus' inner circle was Peter, James and John because Luke clearly identifies them as the only ones invited in. On a number of occasions in the Gospels we see them included, and the other disciples excluded, which might have ignited some frustration and tension. But when you're in a crisis, you need people around you who will nudge you towards faith and trust and not drain you and make things worse!

Those mocking wailers were not given access to witness the miracle of Jairus' daughter being raised either – perhaps this was partly because, at this stage, Jesus did not want news of the miracle to be widespread. But also when focus was needed to deal with the power of death, sneering observers would not be helpful. Do you know who your friends are, and who can stand with you to help you change, or hold your hand through a winter season?

Prayer: Father, help me to prayerfully identify those who are truly my friends, that I might invest in our relationships. Amen.

Astonished

Read:
Mark 5:41–42
Mark 7:31–37

FOCUS

'At this they were completely astonished.'
(Mark 5:42)

I was talking recently to a Baptist minister friend about what he calls a 'midlife faith crisis'. It's a frequent issue. We decide to follow Jesus, and feel great excitement and anticipation at the beginning. We're enthusiastic about sharing the good news, and throw ourselves into serving our local church. Worship is a joy; Bible study an exploration of discovery. But then, years pass, and we begin to settle. Church is a habit rather than a joy. We've become familiar with Bible truth, and have stopped digging for more. And prayer is dutiful, but not very expectant. In short, Jesus no longer seems astonishing.

As Jesus takes the little girl's hand, He isn't worrying about being made ritually unclean by touching a dead body. Just as He was untroubled by the touch of that 'unclean' woman, so He continues to initiate contact, and then speaks a gentle word of command. The words He uses could be translated, 'little girl', 'little lady', or 'little lamb'. Immediately, life flows into the corpse, and she obeys Him. And the response of the witnesses is total, complete astonishment – the word used is *ecstase* from which we get our word 'ecstatic'.

I don't want to be addicted to the exciting, but I do want to ask God to show me more of His character, and enable me to see more of His power. Settling into sameness is not a good idea. I'd like my first love back, although first love is not first faith. More about that tomorrow.

Prayer: Renew my capacity to be surprised by You, Lord. Show me more of Your amazing self. Amen.

Renew my capacity to be surprised by You

Looking back, moving forward

Before we take a final look at this beautiful episode, let's pause for a moment. When we think of new beginnings, our tendency is to look forward to something different. But God has always made looking back an intrinsic part of renewal. The feasts and festivals that were instituted for Israel gave God's people the opportunity to look back at their history, and remember and celebrate what God had done. But looking back also nudged them to look at their lives in the present: how were they doing as people of covenant, with responsibilities to obey the Lord and walk with Him? Remembrance provoked evaluation and fresh commitment, and the potential of a better future.

I mentioned yesterday that I do want my first love for Jesus back, but not my first faith. There's a difference. I don't want my thoughtless, naive faith back, or my nervousness about asking questions. But I do want my first love – commitment, willingness to risk, expectation and then, as we saw yesterday, the capacity still to be astonished by Jesus. I want child-like, not childish faith. May it be so.

To ponder: What is the difference between first love and first faith for you?

Remembrance provoked...
fresh commitment

Extraordinary and ordinary mingled

FOCUS

'He gave strict orders
not to let anyone
know about this,
and told them to
give her something
to eat.' (Mark 5:43)

All this talk of newness and change could give us the false impression that faith is an exciting hop, skip and jump from one exhilarating experience to another. Some believers seem to imply they spend their days receiving continual revelations from God, and rush with unseemly haste to declare a person has been healed when perhaps a doctor's diagnosis to confirm a miracle would be prudent. Following Jesus has its exciting moments, but we walk by faith in the world of the mundane.

One can only imagine the dizzy hysteria that filled the room as a daughter, mourned by loud wailing moments earlier, was now restored to life. Perhaps in their hearts, her parents had already begun to try to adjust to the idea that they would never see her smile again. And now she was alive! What an amazing atmosphere of reunion was in that room. But in the excitement, not only did Jesus tell all present to keep news of this miracle to themselves (the time was not right for more public declarations about His identity as Messiah) but He also had to remind them to prepare a meal for her. Death had made her hungry. Although the command of Jesus restarted her heart, it didn't fill her stomach, and so this story ends with a mingling of the extraordinary and the ordinary, the divine and the deeply practical. And that is a portrait of the Christian life. Jesus has washed my sins away, but I still have to wash the car. Come to think of it, I'd better take care of that right now...

Prayer: Father, sometimes this is all I know: 'The Lord Almighty is with me; the God of Jacob is my fortress' (Psa. 46:11). Amen.

A terrifying situation

Read:
Mark 5:1–6
Mark 4:35–41

FOCUS

'When he saw Jesus from a distance, he ran and fell on his knees in front of him.' (Mark 5:6)

As we turn now to another episode of radical change we need to set the scene. Jesus' disciples were already afraid – and this event wouldn't have helped that. Having a screaming, naked chap charging at them would not have been good for their nerves. The disciples had been terrified because of the storm, and then traumatised by what Jesus did in the midst of it. The word used in Mark 4:41 means they feared 'a great fear'. They were tired. The sea was calm because Jesus had calmed it (that was the good news) but a becalmed boat meant they had to row the rest of the way. It was late in the evening, in that time that Leo Rosten calls 'the dark colony of the night', when shadows threaten and problems grow. They were also tense because they were in foreign territory, the land of the Gerasenes, an area inhabited mainly by Gentiles, who been given freedom from Jewish domination by the Romans about 70 years earlier. To cap it all, they were in a graveyard area. But all that is about to change.

As this frightening event began, I'm sure the disciples' instinct, based on the options to fight or run away, would be to flee, to get out of that location as soon as possible. But Jesus was about to do a work of change. I've mentioned before that I am writing this in the midst of the coronavirus pandemic. Fear abounds. I want it to end. But I also want to retain the lessons I've learned and (hopefully) the maturity gained from this scary time. Change often comes in the shadowy times.

Prayer: I don't want to waste the time when trial comes, Father, but learn, grow and be changed in them by Your Spirit. Amen.

From chained to changed

I've written about Gram Seed before, but his story of radical change has been such an inspiration to me. Once a violent football hooligan and debt enforcer (you can read his story in *One Step Beyond*, available from CWR), Gram is one of the kindest, most gentle people that I've met. We have spent time together, travelling in ministry, so I have had the opportunity to see him up close. He was once without hope, but now is changed forever. When homeless and near death, he responded to Jesus and now everything is different. His character bears no resemblance to the man that he was.

This story of the man possessed by demons is one of utter despair. He has no dignity, running around naked. He is violent, the terror of the whole locality. Covered in blood and scars, he yells out a scream of despair. The word here means a shriek and, in ancient Greek plays, was used to describe the throaty screams of frogs. He is a captive, specifically to demonic powers. His pain is continuous, and he is tormented night and day. His plight has shattered all of his relationships; he lives among the tombs, ostracised and rejected. No one and nothing are strong enough to subdue him. Ironically, he has an illusion of strength, breaking chains but he couldn't break free of the invisible power that ruled him.

No hope. But then Jesus came by. He is the freedom fighter.

Prayer: Lord, nothing is too hard for You. Help me to remember that when I am tempted to give up praying for someone. Amen.

Read:
Mark 5:1–6
Jeremiah 32:17

FOCUS

'Night and day among the tombs and in the hills he would cry out and cut himself with stones.' (Mark 5:5)

Jesus... the freedom fighter

We are 'His business'

Read:
Mark 5:7–13
Luke 5:1–11

FOCUS

'He shouted at the top of his voice, "What do you want with me, Jesus, Son of the Most High God? In God's name don't torture me!"'
(Mark 5:7)

It's a bewildering picture. The demoniac shouts mingled words of praise and resistance. On the one hand, he declares the identity of Jesus as Son of the Most High God, but then he begs Jesus not to torture him. The words he uses, 'What do you want with me?' carry the sense of 'Mind your own business!'

In a sense, although his need was extreme, the man is a picture of us all. We know our need of Jesus, but then at times we resist Him. In the Garden of Eden, the serpent is deceptive, maligning the character of God, suggesting that He is not good. That whisper continues, as the enemy tries to convince humanity that God is oppressive. The man is tortured by the presence of the demonic, but fears that Jesus will be the source of more torture!

We see the cunning of Satan here too. The demons compel the man to use Jesus' name. It was thought that knowing the name of a demon helped in its exorcism; and notice that Jesus demanded that the demons name themselves. Conversely, it was also thought that their knowing the name of the exorcist would hinder the exorcist's authority. Despite all this confusion, Jesus presses in to bring liberation to this distraught man, and at last, the demonic intruders are expelled.

Jesus is the liberator, the life-giver, the source of joy. And wonderfully, we are His business, loved and seen by Him. Or in the words of Peter, who also once asked Jesus to go away, 'He cares for you' (1 Pet. 5:7).

we are...
loved and
seen by Him

Prayer: I am the object of Your care and love, Father. I am Your concern. I gladly welcome Your work in my life. Amen.

Please leave, Jesus

A s we've been thinking about change in this edition of *Life every Day*, we've seen that although God is the agent of transformation, He calls us to co-operate with Him. We are not puppets in His hand; we can choose. This episode ends with the locals making an awful decision to ask Jesus to go away. Picture the scene – the man who had been naked was clothed; his dignity restored. Previously a raging menace, now he had self-control. Jesus had solved their problem. All their previous efforts had been unsuccessful but now, perhaps driven by superstition, prejudice, or financial self-interest, they ask Him to leave. Once again, there's irony here, because the man who initially screamed at Jesus to leave him alone is whole, while the 'respectable' people want nothing to do with Him.

Some people say that they would follow Jesus if they could only witness a mighty miracle. Let God prove His existence, they say, and then we'll embrace Christianity. But these local residents had witnessed the stunning transformation of a man who had been a notorious problem. Their attempts to restrain him with chains show that his condition had created fear and disruption. Now he sits quietly, a living demonstration of the mighty power of God. Despite this, Jesus is given His marching orders.

As followers of Christ, we all come to junction moments, crises of obedience. Will we keep in step with Him, or break away to follow our own agendas? Today, let's choose well.

Prayer: When tempted to wander and even refuse You, Jesus, grant me clarity to choose You and Your way. Amen.

FRI 19 FEB

Read:
Mark 5:14–17
John 14:15–21

FOCUS

'Then the people began to plead with Jesus to leave their region.' (Mark 5:17)

Read:
Mark 5:18–20
Mark 3:13–15

Go home to your family

It is perhaps natural for the previously demonised man, overwhelmed by Jesus' power and compassion, to want to go with Him, perhaps to join His team. This was more than a desire to serve – the wording used means simply 'to be with Him'. Jesus doesn't just want our service, but our company. The disciples were not only called to go out to preach, but to be 'with Him'.

We might think that the idea of a former demoniac being on the team would have been a good one. But in this case, the request was turned down because there was work for him to do in the Decapolis area. The man was called to serve in his own locality. His testimony was met with amazement, although this doesn't mean that the people of that region became followers of Jesus.

Notice Jesus' tenderness: He tells the man to 'Go home to your own people' (Mark 5:19). The reference to going home is picked up by some commentators, suggesting Jesus was encouraging the man to enjoy the family life that he had lost due to his previous torment. In leading us into change, God knows us and what we need.

To ponder: Do you share with friends and family how much Jesus has done for you?

God knows us

Mission Possible

In Antioch, believers scattered by persecution gathered with other refugees and migrants to create one of the greatest churches in history. Here Paul began his ministry, making it his base for his missionary journeys. In the next issue of *Life Every Day*, let's learn from this amazing church that God's mission for us today is totally possible!

Also available as eBook/eSubscription

Obtain your copy from Waverley Abbey Resources, Christian bookshops or your National Distributor. If you would like to take out a subscription, see the order form at the back of these notes.

We *can* change

FOCUS

'And if the Spirit of him who raised Jesus from the dead is living in you, he who raised Christ from the dead will also give life to your mortal bodies'
(Rom. 8:11)

I have a confession. I have been personally challenged as we've reflected on newness and change, and I'm asking the question – am I still changing and growing, four decades after deciding to follow Jesus? Rather than considering another Bible character, I'd like us to ponder a few summary statements that I hope will encourage us to keep journeying with the God who is committed to bring renewal into our lives.

The first is this: let's know that we *can* change. The stories of transformation that we've looked at give ample testimony to the truth that, with Jesus in our lives, we don't have to surrender to sameness. When bad habits turn into addictions, we can feel trapped, and hope for freedom fades. Negative attitudes creep in, spoiling our relationships, and when others make us aware that we're out of order, we insist, 'It's just the way I am. It's too late for me to change now.' But that's a lie. The power that caused a little girl to get up from her deathbed, and raised Christ from the dead after three days in the tomb – that same power of the Holy Spirit is available to us and at work within us. Ultimately, we will experience resurrection and victory over death through the work of the Spirit, but now, the Holy Spirit wants to shape us as we co-operate with God. Today, I am asking the Lord to show me areas of my life that He wants to work on – especially areas that I've just tacitly accepted and settled into. Why not join me?

Prayer: I am not what I was, but I do not want to stay where I am. Change my heart, stir me from any settling, Mighty God. Amen.

Faith is a daily choice

TUES 23 FEB

Read:
Matthew 6:9–13
Matthew 6:25–34

FOCUS
*'Give us today our
daily bread.'*
(Matt. 6:11)

As a teenager, attending an annual Christian youth camp on the Isle of Wight was a real lifeline for me. Mornings were spent in Bible studies, afternoons in sport, and evenings in worship and celebration. Night after night I would go forward for prayer; it was like a fast track to growth and maturity. Later, I would be privileged to help lead Spring Harvest, which attracted many thousands for days of teaching and worship. Countless decisions were made during those times, as people were converted, challenged and comforted. I really believe that events like these can help us to grow and change. But we should realise that change comes, not just in the occasional event or even weekly church service, but in the daily choice to follow Christ. There's a special temptation for those who are part of large and exciting churches to live off Sunday's corporate atmosphere, but not to develop the strong personal walk with God that is necessary on a Monday morning.

Jesus surely teaches us that faith is a day-by-day journey. We are instructed to ask for *daily* bread, and when we're tempted to be anxious about the future, we're reminded that each day has enough trouble of its own. The resolve that I lived in yesterday may fade when I'm tempted today. So while events, conferences and church services can help us to keep growing, let's know that slow, gradual change happens as, with each new dawn, we choose to walk by faith with Jesus.

Prayer: Today, Lord, is all I have. The past is gone, tomorrow is not guaranteed. Today, I choose You. Work in me. Amen.

with each
new dawn...
choose to
walk by faith

Abiding produces fruit

Read:
John 15:1–17
Galatians 5:22–23

FOCUS

'I am the vine; you are the branches. If you remain in me and I in you, you will bear much fruit; apart from me you can do nothing.'
(John 15:5)

I've often been both encouraged and troubled by the call Jesus gives us to 'abide' in Him. He shows us that if real change is going to happen, then we need to do this. Just as a branch cannot produce grapes unless it is connected to the vine as its source, so Jesus is the source of real change in our lives. Paul repeats the idea as he talks to the Christians in Galatia about the fruit of the Holy Spirit. But what does it mean to abide? I find lengthy prayer challenging, but have lived with the impression that I need a mystical life of union with Jesus, a continual state of prayer – and that's never been possible for me. While prayer is obviously vital – it sits at the heart our relationship with God – abiding is not about maintaining a spiritual posture. The Greek word *meno* means 'to stay with'. It was used by the two disciples who asked Jesus where He was staying (John 1:38–40). To abide is to reside, to remain with. Abiding is about being connected, dependent and continuing in our relationship with Christ. We will grow as we nurture our relationship with Jesus, knowing our provision and purpose come from Him – and then, just keep on keeping on. Brian Hedges says: 'Abiding means keeping the words of Jesus in our hearts and minds, so that they are renewing and reviving us, shaping and sanctifying us, filling and forming us. And it means keeping ourselves in his infinite, enduring, sin-bearing, heart-conquering, life-giving love.'*

Prayer: Lord, I want to live today with You, through You, Your Spirit producing good fruit in me for the Father's glory. Amen.

*Brian Hedges, 'What does it mean to abide in Christ?', posted March 2014, taken from christianity.com [Accessed June 2020]

WAVERLEY ABBEY

Find out more online

For more information and to make purchases of new books and courses or to take a look at the college courses and training that we offer, please take a look at our websites.

 waverleyabbey.org

 waverleyabbeyresources.org

 waverleyabbeycollege.ac.uk

 waverleyabbeyhouse.org

What about the plank?

Read:
Matthew 7:3–6
James 1:22–25

FOCUS

'Why do you look at the speck of sawdust in your brother's eye and pay no attention to the plank in your own eye?' (Matt. 7:3)

In today's focus verse, Jesus painted a portrait of a hapless chap, running around armed with a magnifying glass, keen to identify specks of sawdust in the eyes of others, but oblivious to the whacking great plank sticking out from his own head. Apparently, this 'log' would have been the main support for a house, about 12 metres long, a significant protrusion. And people do act like this, especially in churches. Fault-finding souls, eager to catch people doing or believing something suspect, they patrol around searching for someone or something to correct. When they find something that appears to be amiss, they pounce on it with unseemly joy, thrilled by yet another opportunity to highlight a problem. At times, their attitudes are far worse than the issue they are determined to correct, but they remain blissfully unaware of this. Perhaps some take up fault-finding as a hobby in order to spare themselves the discomfort of self-discovery. Peering at others through a magnifying glass is so much easier than staring at ourselves in a mirror.

If we're in the habit of locating sawdust specks, perhaps it's time to focus more on what we're often blind to – our own faults and foibles. Next time we're tempted to get irate about the speck of sawdust lingering in our brother's eye, let's check that we're not carting around a large plank in our own. If we don't, we'll never change.*

Prayer: Father, show me what I don't see about me, when I am tempted to focus on what is wrong with others rather than my own sins. Amen.

*Abridged from Jeff Lucas, *Specks and Planks* (Farnham, Surrey: CWR, 2020)

Work it out

have never been comfortable with that little phrase, 'Let go and let God.' The impression is that we have to do little when it comes to spiritual formation – just leave it to God. But the Bible is filled with calls to intentional living, commands that we be alert and disciplined. Here Paul calls the Philippians to work out their salvation. This is not working *for* our salvation (that would be contrary to everything Paul says about salvation being a free gift) but working it out, considering what God wants from us, applying discipline in our lives – the implications of being saved.

Paul's next statement points us to the source of our power – God working in us. This working out is what Eugene Peterson called a 'long obedience in the same direction'. Again, we see the principle of partnership with the Lord as He works to produce fruit and growth. The writer to the Hebrews celebrates this: 'Now may the God of peace... equip you with everything good for doing his will, and may he work in us what is pleasing to him, through Jesus Christ, to whom be glory for ever and ever. Amen' (Heb. 13:20–21).

Often, we focus on the inner struggles we have when tempted, but fail to acknowledge that, when the Spirit of God is at work, there will be an inner impulse to do what is right. It's wonderful when, coming to a moral crossroads, we suddenly *want* to do what is right. That is God at work in us, so let's keep working out what He's working in!

Prayer: Thank You for Your commitment to continue to work in me, Father. May I respond quickly to all that You are doing. Amen.

Read:
Philippians 2:12–13
Hebrews 13:20–21

FOCUS
'Continue to work out your salvation with fear and trembling, for it is God who works in you.'
(Phil. 2:12–13)

let's keep working out what He's working in!

The day is coming

I'm not very good at finishing projects, especially those that bore me. I made the mistake of ordering something online that required self-assembly, a phrase that strikes terror in my heart. I want the finished product, not the assembly process.

Thankfully, God does not have that kind of attitude when it comes to bringing change and growth in our lives. Paul promises the Christians in Philippi that 'He who began a good work in you will carry it on to completion until the day of Christ Jesus' (Phil. 1:6). And what a day that will be! Not only will we see Him face to face, but we shall be like Him, promises the beloved disciple John. Think of that – the lifelong project will be over, the journey done. We who once wrestled with temptation, slipped into failure and were so inconsistent – we will bear the total, complete family likeness of our big brother, Jesus. In the meantime, today is another day, so… let's keep moving forward with Him by faith.

To ponder: Imagine what it will be like to be like Christ. Let's commit ourselves afresh to the onward journey.

what a day that will be… we
shall be like Him

weekend